Elephants and Their Trunks

Written by Michèle Dufresne

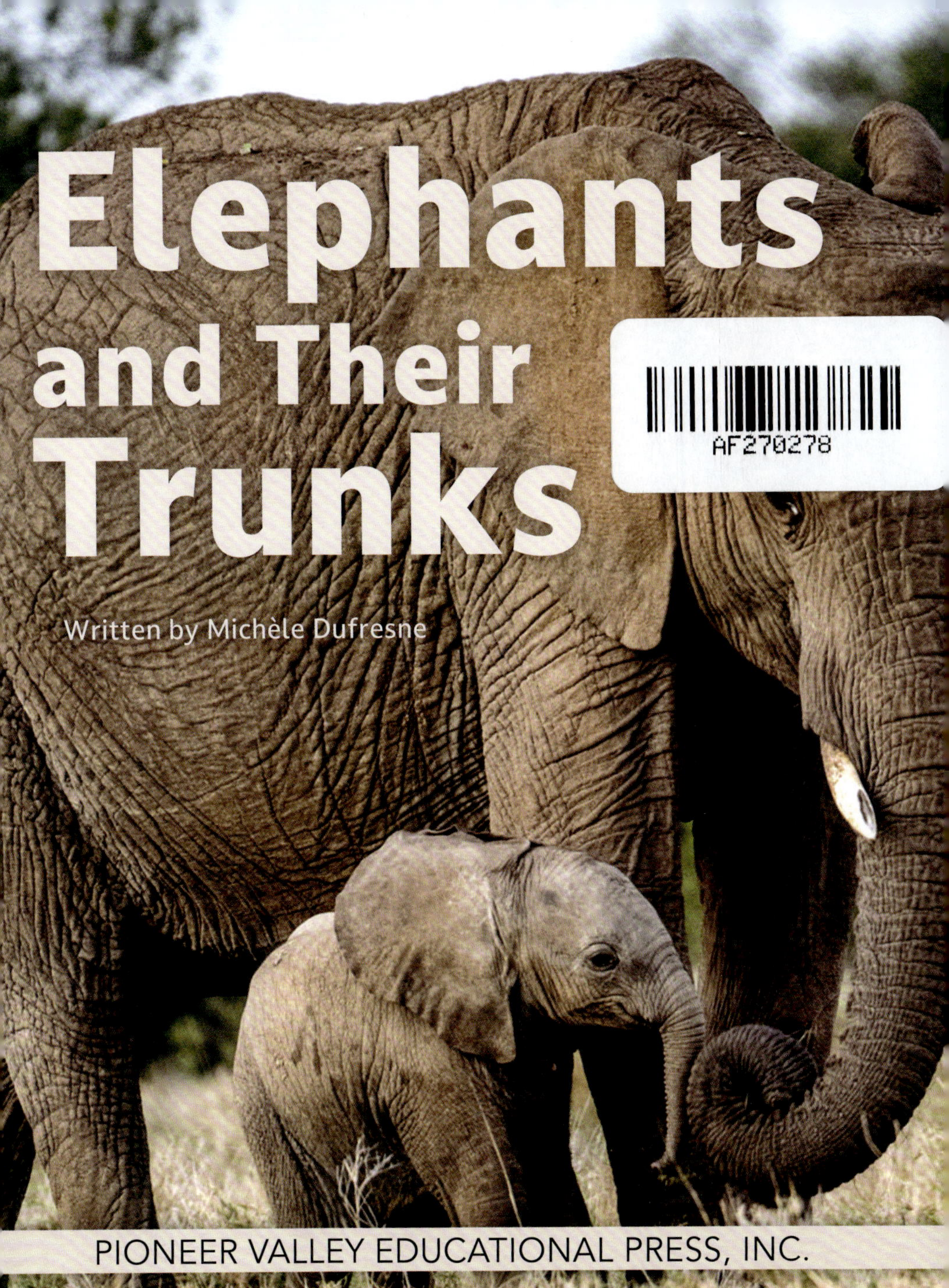

PIONEER VALLEY EDUCATIONAL PRESS, INC.

Here is an **elephant**. Elephants are big. They can stomp on a stump.

An African elephant can weigh up to 7 tons. African elephants are the largest animals that live on land.

Elephants have long trunks. An elephant can grab a snack with its trunk.

An elephant trunk is both an upper lip and a nose. The trunk is very strong.

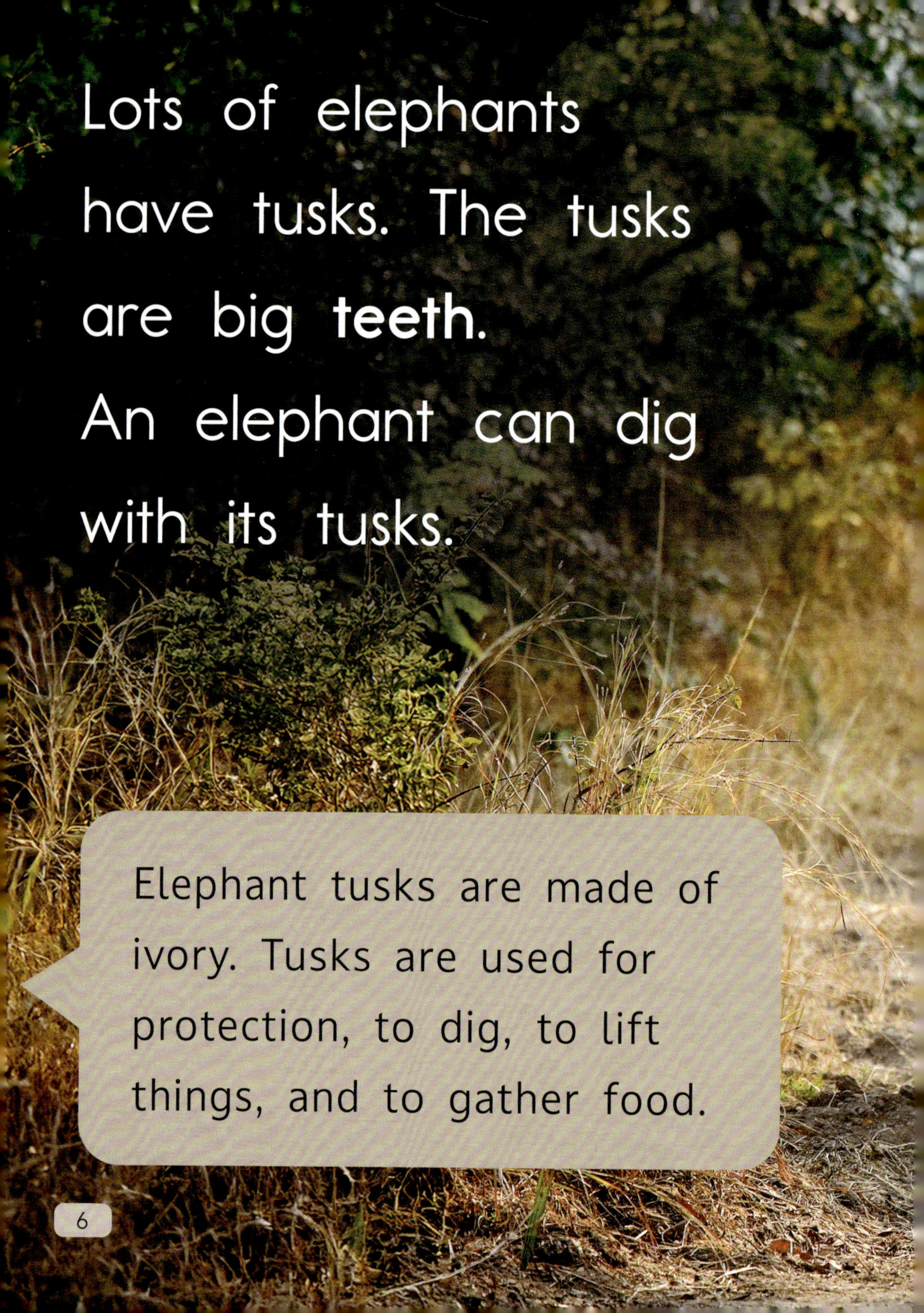

Lots of elephants have tusks. The tusks are big **teeth.**

An elephant can dig with its tusks.

Elephant tusks are made of ivory. Tusks are used for protection, to dig, to lift things, and to gather food.

Elephants can swim. Look! The elephants have swum up and down the **river**.

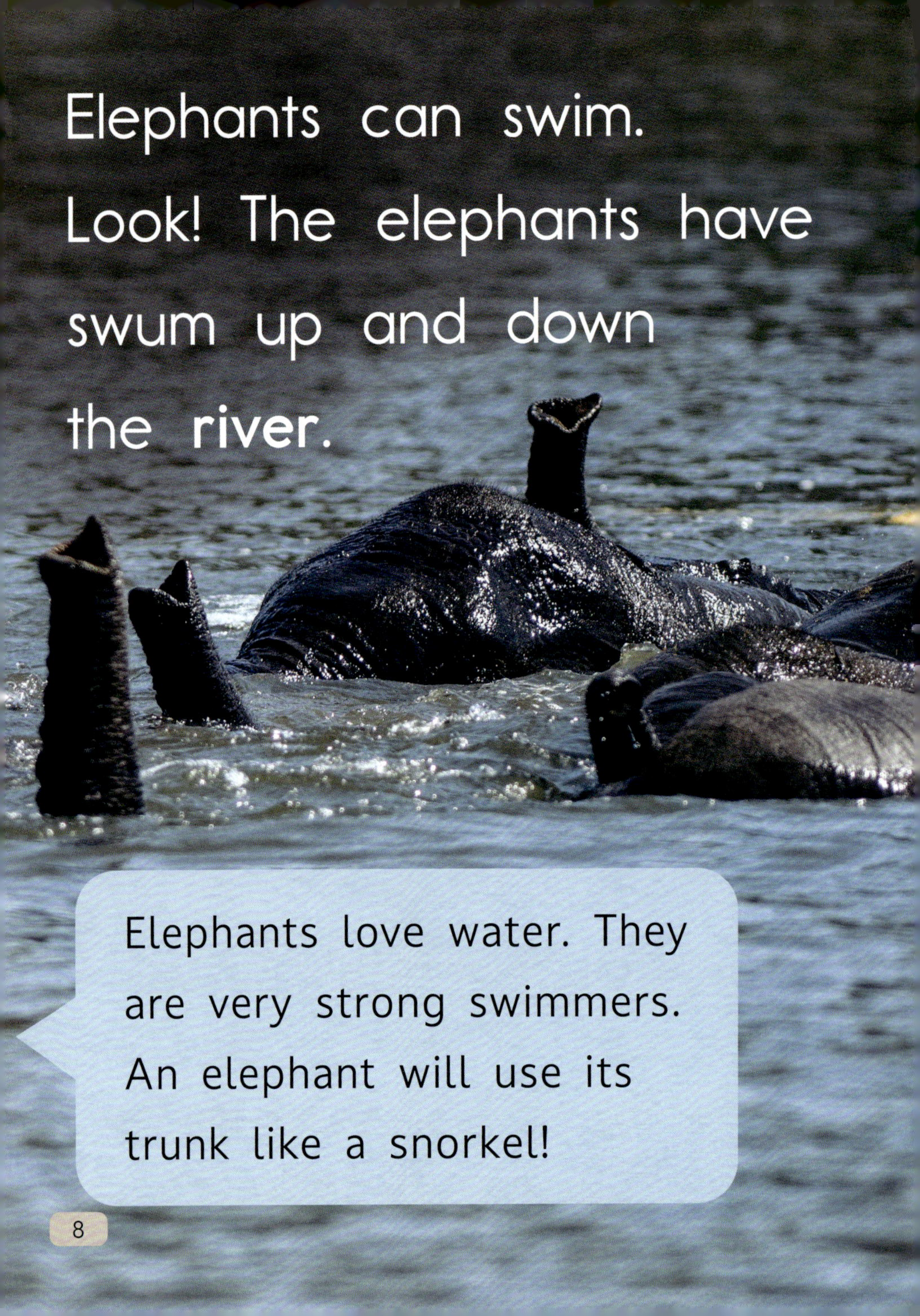

Elephants love water. They are very strong swimmers. An elephant will use its trunk like a snorkel!

An elephant can be glum.

Scientists have found that elephants have deep feelings. They show happiness, sadness, and love.

Look at the **baby** elephant. It is snug with its mom.

A baby elephant is called a calf. Calves stay very close to their mothers.

glossary

elephant

teeth

river

baby